T0046203

PRAISE FOR CATHERINE GRAHAM

Æther: An Out-of-Body Lyric
2021

Winner of the 2022 Fred Kerner Book Award
Finalist for the 2022 Trillium Book Award
Finalist for the 2021 Toronto Book Awards

"*Æther* entwines in poetry as well as prose a deeply explored experience of surviving life and death as a daughter and as an adult. This book-length poetic essay gifts us with a personal account of the precious mundanities of healing along with the guilt and joy of being alive longer than our parents. With poetic delicacy counterpointed by plain speaking, *Æther* never shirks from the realities we must all face if we are to see the experience of living through to the end." – Fred Kerner Book Award, judges' comments

"Catherine Graham's seventh book of poetry is an intricate reverie, in poetry and prose, which floats back and forth in time and between memories, dreams and reflections." – Barb Carey, *Toronto Star*

"Part poetry, part prose, *Æther: An Out-of-Body Lyric* by Catherine Graham is a wonderfully unconventional read. More than a memoir of a breast cancer survivor, Graham writes from that in-between world of soft wakefullness and dreaming during post-op recovery at Toronto's Princess Margaret Hospital. In this state, dreams become memories and memories become clarity. For anyone who has undergone surgery, they can easily identify with the way Graham has penned this personal narrative. *Æther* is an engaging work and a unique experience." – Toronto Book Awards, jury citation

"It is a masterpiece. . . . The melding of poetry and prose into a beautiful and heartbreaking skein, gradual revelation, going back/going forward, weaving in and out, repeating and broadening the meaning as you go. A journey that is fascinating, heartrending, and courageous." – Marilyn Gear Pilling, author of *The Gods of East Wawanosh*

"It illustrates how, through writing painful experiences, trauma may be 'owned' and redirected into nurturance, creativity and a gift to readers. A gorgeous achievement." – Kathleen McCracken, author of *Double Self Portrait with Mirror: New and Selected Poems*

The Celery Forest
2017

Finalist for the Fred Cogswell Award for Excellence in Poetry

"An impressive new collection, *The Celery Forest* is both powerful and beautiful, a work of great fortitude and invention, full of jewel-like moments and dark gnomic utterances. It faces into the dark and finds a way through." – Michael Longley, author of *The Stairwell*

"*The Celery Forest* is a book of enacted grace, poetic resourcefulness, and imaginative courage. It is also, regarding its subject and its author's experience, a genuine and intensely compelling work of art." – Robert Wrigley, author of *Anatomy of Melancholy and Other Poems*

"*The Celery Forest* is a volume of poems wrought mainly in language that (like the language of Wallace Stevens, for example) is brilliantly and intriguingly circuitous." – P.W. Bridgman, *Glasgow Review of Books*

"*The Celery Forest* is a wild book with all its physical and metaphysical fears and tastes of absurdity. . . . Undefined, ambiguous as in a dream, difficult to understand who, where and what, the elements seem to be projected from a source outside. It's a special psychological position, more than a stylistic choice, bringing a new order and re-dimensioning of things." – Luljeta Lleshanaku, author of *Negative Space*

"*The Celery Forest* is a fantastical world with strange creatures and disorienting sights. Within the poetry collection's magical imagery is the examination of Catherine Graham's recent bout with breast cancer; the novelist and poet uses sensual language and style that peers into the duality of beauty and horror." – CBC Books, "The Best Canadian Poetry of 2017"

"Such a beautiful book, where every bird, cell and syllable counts. After a few reads I found myself approaching it like one long poem rather than a collection of shorter pieces. Catherine lets the weight of her subject matter bend, break and expand her lines wonderfully. The craft of her poetry is far, far stronger than the cancer she survived." – Patrick Woodcock, author of *You Can't Bury Them All*

Her Red Hair Rises with the Wings of Insects
2013

Finalist for the Raymond Souster Award for Poetry
Finalist for the Canadian Authors Association Award for Poetry

"The experimental entrances into Dorothy Molloy's poems are fascinating. I adore form and fiddling with it, and Graham shows what can happen when one reads a deceased poet's work so deeply that their spirit in a sense infiltrates, shaping not only the content, but more importantly, the structure of the work." – Catherine Owen, *Relentless Adventures of OCD Crow* (blog)

"Graham's poems are sparely worded but full of evocative images that vividly convey a wide range of emotion, from passion to grief." – CBC Books

"Graham's fifth poetry collection, *Her Red Hair Rises with the Wings of Insects*, began as a deliberate experiment that turned gothic and magical." – George Elliott Clarke, *The Chronicle Herald*

"There is humour, wit, sensual experience, fantasy and grace in these poems. Hard to ask for more than that. It is also a delight to read, to recommend." – Michael Dennis, *Michael Dennis Poet* (blog)

"The elegant fifth collection of poetry by Catherine Graham is an experiment gone right. . . . A master of vivid imagery, Graham evokes all the senses, allowing readers to bask along the way in both the beauty and horror of the world." – Jessica Rose, *This Magazine*

"Graham offers no easy answers, and what at first looks like defeatism and resignation in the face of pain gives way to a hard-won acceptance." – Anouk H. Henri, *Arc Poetry Magazine*

"While the original idea for the collection was formed using the straightjacket restraint, the final poems blossomed out of a resistant and creative freedom. The final product is subtly violent and beautifully poetic." – *Contemporary Verse 2*

"Catherine Graham is the über-maestro of whipping up images that startle, surprise and delight . . . she lays bare all our desires, fears and hopes. She shows how we are sculpted by society, how our intellects are forced into cookie cutter molds and yet the characters in her poems resist this forced shaping and they speak with their own voices, voices that are unforgettable and brutally pure." – Brick Books' Celebration of Canadian Poetry

Winterkill
2010

"From unicorns to frogs and turtles to moths, Graham utilizes images from fantasy and nature, working these poems to mine a quarry of loss: 'We look for the dead in the living.' And Graham writes that loss into startling poems." – *The Telegraph-Journal*

"Graham invests the colours red and green with layers of meaning to the point that it verges on self-induced synesthesia. But the repetition of this and other motifs (wings, water) is incantatory – and effective." – Ariel Gordon, *Winnipeg Free Press*

"The gifts they offer are expansive and reward close attention . . . that's the beauty of this and so many other poems in Winterkill: you're given lots of space to fill in the blanks on your own . . . Winterkill is a warm, generous and welcoming collection of poems." – Mark Sampson, *Free Range Reading* (blog)

"Catherine Graham's poems are at once delicate and terrifying. . . . My favourite poetry is the narrative kind, and Catherine tells such incredibly layered stories with so few words that I'm constantly blinking in amazement." – Jessica Westhead, *The New Quarterly*

"As the last of Graham's Quarry Trilogy, *Winterkill* will surely leave on the reader's fingertips a residue of sleek creek mud, of purifying snowdrifts, and the bittersweet cadence of self and loss." – Caitlin Galway, *The Toronto Quarterly*

"Another highly accessible collection of poetry from one of Toronto's brightest poetry minds." – *Open Book: Toronto*

"Desire, menace and loss thrum through this collection of deceptively restrained, brief poems that, in the main, mourn the early deaths of the poet's parents. Imagery of mysterious creatures (a misunderstood troll, a unicorn wearied by expectations, the trickster rabbit of a breakfast cereal), the natural world of vivid colours and decay, and a dream-like abandoned quarry indirectly expresses both the poignancy of grief and a wild, just-below-the-surface longing . . . these are works of supple strength that have emerged from the storm to linger in the mind." – Kateri Lanthier, *Advent Book Blog*

"Catherine Graham is a poet of the intimate voice, the treasured, internalised experience." – *Parameter Magazine* (UK)

The Red Element
2008

"In her stunning new volume of poems, *The Red Element*, Catherine Graham distills the whirling ambiguities of memories into gorgeous, mysterious single images, making the short poem triumph again on the Canadian literary landscape. With the dense, new energy of *The Red Element*, where all the poems form a bravura lyrical sequence, Graham proves herself as one of Canada's premier younger poets." – Molly Peacock

"These poems are fine works." – George Elliott Clarke, *The Chronicle Herald*

"More goose bumps per page than any collection in recent memory. Sticking to the poetic doctrine less is more, this collection is a tour de force in minimalism. Her steady hand and firm voice are breathtaking. They are empowered images, graceful sparks." – Angela Hibbs, *Broken Pencil*

"These poems are sharp, imaginative, and never cutesy . . . Graham's poetry is especially admirable in its combination of accessibility, urgency, and imagination, making *The Red Element* one of my favourite poetry collections of the year." – Hannah Stephenson, *Gloss*

"Having carved out her particular niche on the Canlit map with her last two offerings, *The Watch* and *Pupa, The Red Element* is another groundbreaking delight." – *Scene Magazine*

"It is worthwhile to let *The Red Element* suck you into its vividly morbid world." – *Matrix*

"The oneiric surrealism engendered there is highly effective; it harnesses narrative purpose and stanza order in tension to the seemingly random menace of the poems' imagery." – *Arc Poetry Magazine*

Pupa
2003

"The poems in *Pupa*, her first collection, are spiky little meditations so taut and tightly controlled they are almost claustrophobic . . . The poems' effect is all the more intense as a result. . . . This impressive collection should put her on the Canlit map." – *Toronto Star*

"The best advice that I can give on this book is to go read it, let Graham explain Graham to you." – *Grey Borders*

"Graham is a young poet whose work should be closely attended to." – *Arc Poetry Magazine*

"Graham's *Pupa* is a debut collection of graceful concision and surprising wisdom." – *The Times-Colonist*

"Her best work is at once brief, yet resonant . . . the sophistication of their brevity, remind me of Roethke." – M. Travis Lane, *The Fiddlehead*

put flowers

around us

and

pretend

we're

dead

Also by Catherine Graham

POETRY

The Celery Forest
Her Red Hair Rises with the Wings of Insects
Pupa
Put Flowers Around Us and Pretend We're Dead: New and Selected Poems
The Red Element
The Watch
Winterkill

FICTION

The Most Cunning Heart
Quarry

HYBRID

Æther: An Out-of-Body Lyric

put flowers

around us

and

pretend

we're

dead

Catherine
Graham

new and
selected poems

© Catherine Graham, 2023

No part of this publication may be reproduced, stored in a retrieval system or transmitted, in any form or by any means, without the prior written consent of the publisher or a license from the Canadian Copyright Licensing Agency (Access Copyright). For an Access Copyright license, visit www.accescopyright.ca or call toll free to 1-800-893-5777.

Published by Buckrider Books
an imprint of Wolsak and Wynn Publishers
280 James Street North
Hamilton, ON L8R2L3
www.wolsakandwynn.ca

Editor for Buckrider Books: Paul Vermeersch | Copy editor: Ashley Hisson
Cover and interior design: Jennifer Rawlinson
Cover image: Martin Johnson Heade, *Orchid and Hummingbird*, 1880
Author photograph: Marion Voysey
Typeset in Minion and Branch
Printed by Coach House Printing Company, Toronto, Canada

The publisher gratefully acknowledges the support of the Ontario Arts Council, the Canada Council for the Arts and the Government of Canada.

Library and Archives Canada Cataloguing in Publication

Title: Put flowers around us and pretend we're dead : new and selected poems / Catherine
      Graham.
Other titles: Poems. Selections
Names: Graham, Catherine (Catherine Marie), author.
Description: Poems.
Identifiers: Canadiana 20230181902 | ISBN 9781989496633 (softcover)
Classification: LCC PS8563.R31452 A6 2023 | DDC C811/.6—dc23

for John Coates

There is more than glass between the snow and the huge roses.

– Louis MacNeice, "Snow"

Contents

Foreword

With the exception of *The Watch*, a beautiful chapbook published in Northern Ireland in 1998, I have worked with Catherine Graham on all of her published collections of poetry to date, beginning with *Pupa* in 2003, followed by *The Red Element* in 2008, *Winterkill* in 2010, *Her Red Hair Rises with the Wings of Insects* in 2013, *The Celery Forest* in 2017 and, most recently, *Æther: An Out-of-Body Lyric* in 2021, a work of hybrid memoir that is not represented in the present volume, but should be seen as a companion to this selection. It has been an honour and a privilege to witness the creation of these books and the evolution of Graham's remarkable lyric voice, a voice that has been frequently, and rightly, praised by critics. Now, with the publication of *Put Flowers Around Us and Pretend We're Dead: New and Selected Poems*, we are invited to look back and take inventory of the ever-expanding world that Graham is creating.

Like other exceptional bodies of work that continually, even obsessively, evolve from a core set of themes and images, Graham's poetry constitutes a kind of parallel reality, a metaphysical reflection of our own, complete with its own logic and laws of nature. Nowhere is this more apparent than in *The Celery Forest*, where Graham's secondary world is named, described in great detail and populated with fantastic creatures like any Narnia, Oz or Wonderland, but the astute reader, looking back, will recognize that the telltale signs of having passed through the looking glass (or wardrobe, or whirlwind, or MRI machine) have been there from the very beginning, even in her first book.

Pupa is the Latin word for *doll*. It also refers to the metamorphic stage, between larva and adult, in the life cycle of many insects – the changing form inside the cocoon, alive but between lives. Doll and metamorphosis – simulacrum and transfiguration – these are themes we now understand to be staples of Graham's work. In the poem "Moths" from her book *Winterkill*, for example, the titular insects beating themselves against the glass to reach the light inside the house are otherworldly manifestations, humans or celestial beings in miniature, beings that suffer grief but are still hell-bent on deliverance, if only they could breach the barrier between worlds that separates them from the light.

1

Like those moths, we find ourselves at the threshold of Graham's inner world, the one just beyond the glass. Long-time readers of her work know this world well and recognize the hallmarks of her literary universe: not just her idols and transmutations, but also her grief and the spectre of death, the loss of her parents and the hauntological intrusion of the past upon the present – in Graham's work often embodied by the image of the quarry near her childhood home, both figuratively and literally, a place of submerged memory – and, more recently, the personal discovery of, and crossing through, the surreal realm of cancer. Unlike those moths, however, we are granted entry into her vast, illuminated world.

We see the further evolution of Graham's themes in the new poems collected in this book, now the latest installment of what is emerging to be Catherine Graham's lifelong project: the celebration of life in the shadow of death, the act of holding one's breath submerged in those memories and, in that quarry, long enough to swim to the surface and breathe.

It is fitting that this book of new and selected poems both prefigures and continues the accomplishments of Graham's previous book, *Æther*. Because it is work of literary autobiography, we find in *Æther* many of the keys to unlocking the doors in Graham's fantastical poetry. *Æther* builds a bridge to her lyrical realm and allows for the return of Graham's obsessions with love and mortality to the physical world.

So what is *Æther*?

It is many things. It is an anesthetic compound that induces a deep, unbreakable slumber. As such, it is the stuff of dreams. It is, in its mythic sense, the substance of which the sky is made and, subsequently, it was believed by nineteenth-century physicists (who found natural vacuums too unthinkable to exist) to be the substance that filled the cosmos and by which light could travel through the universe. It is, in its alchemical sense – after fire, air, earth and water – one of the classical elements. Because in this schema it is the fifth element, it also called *quintessence*, a term that some present-day scientists, in a nod to its classical roots, apply to the phenomenon of dark energy, and from which we take the word *quintessential*, a word that means "representing the most perfect or typical example of a quality or class."

I think, finally, that is how I would describe Catherine Graham's poetry: elemental, celestial, dreamlike, mythic – cosmic even – a medium equally suited to the movement of light and to the presence of a dark energy, and I think, appropriately, quintessential.

I hope you will be moved by it as much I am.

Paul Vermeersch
Toronto
February 2023

put flowers

around us

and

pretend

we're

dead

Consider the Scythian Lamb

We reason about unreasonable things:
the ratio of a hippogryph's
wings to its body, if it can fly.

If the yeti is more likely than elf
to exist when we know
they both don't.

Consider the Scythian Lamb.
Seed breaks through, roots
stalk their slow crawl

into green networks
toward the nourishing air, lengthen
with sun's ease – out climbs a lamb –

hooves made of parted hair.

Horse of Cerberus

My three-ringed prayer
falls flat on its face.

The three hills I slide down
can't escape my shape:

a horse with three heads –
two sprout from my neck.

Look hard enough, the edge
cracks into three songs.

Three tinny crickets
sing the dead back to us

and the oyster of the sun
steals three pearls from the moon.

If Tiny Crystals Form Close to the Earth's Surface They Form Diamond Dust

My antler heart grows hooves.
I follow the footprints of the pack.
Find shelter in a drunken forest –

what species isn't at risk.
Insulating properties of snow
keep me warm –

trapped air between each flake.
With body heat and earth-transfer heat
my home becomes a snowbank.

It's not the hare's scream
that haunts,
it's the antecedent silence.

Field

A field's snow is a ruled wind.
Harnessed, flattened, white gold.

Stalks – stiff.
This brainy circuit breathes beneath.

Sun liquefies ice into steaming puddles.
Sunken grass, soil's green lid thickens.

The call for the flying to come –
transformation's fast hatch.

Walk the field. Feel the grasses tick.
Bend to pluck the frozen thistle.

Take a blade of wind in your teeth.
Whistle.

Star

They don't notice one iris
carries an unbalanced green

or the blue vein snaking
my neck. I'm perfect

in their glare, the filling
light between clicks.

Dark nights, my vacancy
grows. Other nights

I fly through underground springs.
Mornings, my mirror stares back

with such weight, a heavy task
for such a fine-boned thing.

Passage

There you were, floating beneath
before passing through the mist
we could not face. Crabapples,

red-pebbled jewels, rainwater-seeds –
light drying to come out. Yolk,
yellow bubble. Can you hear the singing?

Water falls to where the heart aches,
a ladder slowly lifts and the birds,
the birds hurl themselves up.

Gossip

Grown wild, unkempt hair,
floozy out the dirt –

turn the other cheek, stain-slap
contamination. Balloon moan of her belly.

Ghostbirds

They survive behind light.
The sun's stare blocks their path
                              to not touch.

They hold us like music.
Still, notes push for release –

our goosebumps – quills plucked –
we are all birds beneath.

Map

Take the frog series. Take it.
Talk about your own itches.

With enemy's brightness
you fever a waterfall.

Yes, the lake has teeth.
Respect the lake.

But my divining rod twitches –
late at the strawberry moon.

Child gets lost in dream.
Child stripes of silence.

Daisy. Painted circle
on a stem. Poppy.

Dying is not an abstract art.
Trees talk more than we do.

Fool Room in Maynooth

Pacemakers, peacemakers, he rode to the edge
to be citizen. Wyse beyond his shadow,

he mud-coloured talk into noise
of the night. Plum-eyed, he rolled

about, excited to find the world's
history in one nation –

Ireland –
from gullet to gob –

Here. I was
born here.

Say nothing.
Spit.

Girl with Glass Animals

She will never become their size. Far from the heat
that shaped them, the time that grained them.

Tiny as insects, they fire her imagination. She waits
for her tall Shirley Temple between two missing parents –

Yes to the red brick wall – at recess she stems into a flower
the colour of mother's hair, birds with playground eyes

pin nasty beaks to make her twitch, talk; she keeps
her voice locked, serves only her throat – *monkey, elephant, giraffe*

and as the bird-storm recedes into smaller feather scatters –
ball, hopscotch and skipping rope –

she is far from the heat that shapes her, the time that grains her.

Blue Edges

I took my love for him through burrs in the field, sticky porcupine stars.
What soil am I he keeps plowing? Days the lakeside licked the light
along the beach. We tasted salt in air, in each other's need.

Cakes of light silenced across, our hands moving boundaries.
Rumour dolls up the road cackled to find the devil's claw –
the medieval with their pointy feet. Stiff, rigid cut-outs.

These dreams where I keep losing my purse, the clasp that can't click
a cage around my neck where stars belie whole moons.
An ocean, a quarry – what we can't contain.

The Drifting Experience

We carry mystery as gift. Cloud-along
a tail of soft fog, the scent of this or that.

A star with horns! Or are they antlers?

More woodland souls
sprout green from our wounds.

Moths

In the light hours they burrow.
Walls accept, cracks and

inner crevices welcome.
Something borrowed from another blue,

wind-remnants, a miniature world
tucked in wings, known by rote

from all in flight before them.
Crepe powder, talc, pollen.

When they succumb to *open*
they make the house fly.

Mouthing Birds

All night they land, nest.
My thick locks, source-comfort.
Rachis attaches to root.
I hold what they flutter.

When hair is a house
do we think it strange?
Turning the airborne
into us, feathering highlights.

Out of my mouth they come –
the pea-bead stutter-stop-start
in their hearts makes my tongue
flicker. All day I speak in bird.

All My Blue Januaries

Three of the last-minute Januaries sent me
backwards, dead father. What is there that shines

from another day. Night breathes, saturated
with nevered emptiness, cracks language

into a circle of Sundays. The sun
was something we managed.

Blue-roaming blood, a noose is a necklace
you never got out of. I don't want stars.

Ash is not light. The story is there –
dream-cornered. Leave the necklace

unclasped for the dead. The river has your hands.

Ghost Apples

You are out of the forest now.
Icicle birds, having called, melted.

Ash tree, seen from a distance,
view to underground –

hold flash-happens,
so many goods –

the sleeping mind wants – all of it –
mixing gone with apple's core –

leaving *field* in your bones.

Cassandra

Eyes open to a sun that stuns a gardener's trick –
the concrete frog stifles the croak. Chipped paint, a new pain.

Form in another form hops by. Warts bubble on her hand,
she is a witch in hibernation, the simmered air, her cave.

This fortune-seeing inside-dreams beams yellow riddles,
questions scut exclamation points. Who can be more than whom?

Apple blossoms spit at her face. Fruit splits the aftermath.

The Thread Is What Matters

The frog in the courtyard, a sign.
The moon bulges toward the horizon –
a frog, swallowed. Every

scene holds Ariadne's thread. A maze
we never got out of. That chill
in the open field where the grove

holds no tall yellow willow.
Only a bird remembers, flies
back, hovers. The thread is in her too.

Medusa's Lament

My rage has never belonged to me.

Phallic hisses snake from my scalp,
remind my powers to turn men to stone.

From the deepest marrow, I've become
beauty-uglied. Vital. Fresh.

My mother rose from stone.
Trilobites fossilized her into shape.

Stone, buried want, to be cradled – back –
into her crevice – to be fluid, contained.

Caul Bearers

Blessed. Destined for greatness. Witch.
Killed at birth. Burned at a stake.

Throw us in water, we never drown.
Mythos, lore – more masks that make us.

We see beyond the veil. Attract
energies on a basal level.

Evil comes flying – curse
of the caul. Prayers, spells, rituals.

Strange film – part feather, part
netting – harmless, our first face.

The Unconscious Poem

All the minutes turning burnt orange.
Slippery fixed toward exit, we keep

fishing for birds. The world outside,
packed with goat calves.

Into the robins –
Rabbit has the cutting floor.

If we wake ourselves up
through sleep –

one feather means love.
We are going out

next decade despite
flowers sprouting out of us.

Music Keeper

We were two that used
invisible strings.

Clipped quills on skin,
we made more

many. Taken
to overtaken, a barbed-wire

balance beside a pit
where blood collects.

Music-draped, night slapped
to water pieces –

Not everyone flickers.
Locked, tucked into myself,

I waited to not
be alone.

Never did you hear
my music – beyond reach –

I lost my – *sky* –
fell into words.

Chalk

She lived on a farm in the summit
of a fist – sundress mortality.

To raise the dead we raise
the incision. That flap –

– his fist, her flesh.
Mother, we fill your eyes

with wildflowers.
We chalk you into place.

Wildflower

in memory of Bruce Gillingham, 1929–2019

The condo took him away
from his garden. Pots
on the balcony, not the same.

By the lake, a field with few
wildflowers called to him.
He drove to where the city

kept spreading – holes where
other condos would rise.
Ox-eye daisy, Queen Anne's lace,

butter-and-eggs, chicory –
he transplanted his finds along
the waiting edges. Fox, skunk

and rabbit watched, but not
the passersby as he dug more holes
to root the living. Growth took.

So he planted seeds, nothing invasive,
just more of the already there to richen
texture and colour. Some milkweed

to coax monarchs back. I see
him – tending, tamping, close
to ninety, down on his knees.

Put Flowers Around Us
and Pretend We're Dead

The moon arcs – in and out, playing form.
Stars wrap our fate while intruder dreams
signal: come back. They hold our stability with quickened steps.

Stand where grass weaves basket strands, make
the centre heave, the pinched earth speak,
before thoughts erase and we have no names.

Fixed on the busy you miss the owl-winter, the who-cold
crizzling lake. Raindrops inside snowdrops.
When our shoes sprout hello-flowers, cold lips pucker, speak –

What to do but follow this thread? Wind circular words
to chain our necks. A necklace without clasps
means another light's not listening.

To think story is to construct from that other realm
where jade water cools fire's friction. Pockets where pleasure finds memory.
Take this nosegay, touch intuition, before we float off the page.

Now go past sentence. Air-sheets shatter – absorbed
by grasses and creatures scurrying there.
Viral green points down, we watch the swarm.

Swan's neck quickens to question – her wings,
snow-blinding flaps. Nest birds have it – twiggy cup to sink into
after cracking. The rub that brought forth twine and twig weaves the cradle.

Head naked like a freshly hatched bird, moist with dew from the wormfield.
What moves in tawny spurts, jolts. Silence rearranges. It does not mend.
Seed. But know bloom. Unravelling defies gravity. False to think otherwise.

Fools. We have a future to hatch. When roots shoot out –
the sun-calling art of escape: leaf, sepal, petal – the sun
plays hide-and-seek. Silence is a kind of flight.

Scratch light to a rain-flecked level. Twitch strategic to inhabit submission.
Repetition renews. Upland by the railroad tracks – eggs disguised as stones.
Slip past daylight to a time held by skein of old stars –

past evening, past waiting –
Enough! Never enough, until pulled to flight or sleep.
And a dog bounds helplessly wet for a tossed stick he cannot find.

Haunted

The bow, the arrow,
shadow-pinned, flavoured back.

What shines
from another day?

Robin's abyss,
water-fed head whisky.

The past skies
what heavy fruit holds –

Moonlight.
Things that move in a box.

Songs in the Energy Field

To be famous or liked.
Insisto fashion. Cameo ring.

Who needs treble-clef wisdom?
Songs in the energy field –
condensed, translated.

Here in the fifth-deck series,
a red sun in my purse,
I dream to see wind's wind.

Was I there or did you think
you were? Putting tomorrows
into today. Spiral fork.

Glass-task work. Human
hood's organic purpose –
to shock the field right

out of the house. Music scores
from walls – the way language
curses us. Not the weather

for this channel. The centre
burdens, the ache reaches out –
voices waiting for eyes.

A Person Is Wounded for Every Bird Shot

Ice blossoms – slip
through fingers that don't exist –

wish on my back –
a code for smaller.

Butterfly guardian –
for one big thing –

pincushion my heart: *sing.*

Part of the Song Where the Dead Come From

They dream through us.
Grapes raisin into light, the terroir
glistens in our cups.

Re-entry without thought-want mix –
mind's wax and wane.
We hold the dead's moon.

Full. Not full.
Forever light-trapped.
Framed by Earth's tender angle,

we cart the dead's voices
through our dream-cells –
etches in morning, frostglass.

Spell

Death's physics, a curious trick.
Quarks, leptons, muons.
No sheet
or ghostly tablecloth.
You came as hover.
Music in smoke absence.
Me, alone
in the vinegar hour
as the sun checked down
without sound checks
for pleasure.
The light
you left
rayed into touch.

1964

I'm a sucker punch
for an X-ray star,
streaking power sweep
snowmobiling soundscape.

In my context-free condo
I Indy car an ion channel,
jump jet op art off-the-rack
orientated in my posable pantsuit.

I remaster to strike-slip
the worst-case transfection
or triple jump. Time frame
is a table sugar, this

semipornographic radio collar
quasars a quark. Programmed
cell death, polarity therapy
can't roll cage a rat fink.

Mack daddy's drink-driving
duende's a colour-field – AAA –
black hole, chokehold,
wheel-thrown, worst case.

Composed of words that entered the dictionary in 1964.

Silence

The arc in mother's voice –
tilts
a message to me.

I place it here, in this poem.

Do you feel its breath?
Breathing

from your lungs –

silence

from your mother's voice –
tilt it to me.

Hush

Flight-patterned tea leaves
augur the occasion.
A heart pulled from a yellow
flower bloom pulses.

What quiets the hush?
Deciduous river-shade, scattering
squirrels. Double-take
for the red shed

in memory. Lovers,
from that other realm
where jade water
cools fire's fiction.

Grace Note

Do you see yourself, where the wound
aligns the quicken,

replacing cause, tapping
sounds you can't hear?

Internalize the grace note before moon
strips back, pointing horns.

Night ignites birds into stars
and rain-damp leaves dew for flight.

Sun pulses inside a firefly's abdomen
and crickets twill. A leaf-stuttering

wind flies babies to sleep.
Wait harder for the hills to hollow.

The Many-Eyed Cloud

The weather works its way through our bones,
air, struck from life,
thins by the gesturing sea, the bring cycle.

Let's squeeze sky into rain.
Light,
like all feathers, gathers to make us bird.

The many-eyed cloud with
its crackle-blinks –
we write our way through grief.

Clothes handle
the future now. Blood
once played beneath –

O robin in morning, tree-frogged leaf,
we're as layered
as paper and don't know how to fold.

Parliament of the Invisibles

Alone in the vinegar hour, we ghost the unlived stories.
A feeling thumbprints map, the tender ache, what makes us.

Rotations. Udder clouds.

Nights we ghost in – call it possessed, fever dreams with wildcats,
dream of a plum-black abstract hung in mid-air, titled *Wounds of a Perfect
   Person.*

Flyby orange moth, a perfect leap between sound is leap.

The breath between showers is the sea that dropped us.
Fixed, we know gravity floats. Air is air is feather.

Second-Guessing Is the Beginning

My wound overlaps with rose.
Red, of course, before iron oxidizes.

Cadmium for the circle weft,
disappearance of whom.

Then came *numen, tree
sighting with roots.*

Painted cardinal gates – red birds
made the leap. Name him.

Cunning Folk

Locals say we hoard
omens, tributary
sight from silt and rock.

We keep well
from the hatebox.
Rain slims, winter white –

we pass as eclipse.
That prism in your eyes
grows roses. See?

Ferry Ticket

O spare my wilderness in the middle.
Belonging to the herd. To the ferry. To burn.

Shucked into boxes.
Shadows carried to the yellow flame.

Tones pulled to the window,
even clouds flinch. Blood in an autumn

sun stretches to echo and cold.
Let me forget the withered leaf of your face.

How Does the Groundhog Know?

We're magic not place.
Caress the caregiver, what crisis isn't sick?
Leaving language swift in verbal rain.

Time-revved, the engine berry ripens in the case.
Our brokenness belongs to itself.
Absence twins us to the word-bone.

We trap etheric beneath the tongue.
When death brings back the groundhog, our dreams
swing round the circle itself.

What to do without the minuscule?
Those shivers in the dreambox?
Barefoot, the capital and the grin –

an echo, cut in two, swings by the hedge.
Sun-glitter dusts – to name this –
what's up there in that field?

Hinge

Here in this circle, net as bird's flight stringing invisibles,
I follow the deer trail to plant the ground down.

Before the mound from burning lets ashes
scatter into autumn leaving and winter

hoards the red-eye sun, I recall your legs
dangling at the edge of two worlds.

Thorn Roses

I'll own my own roses
and thorns, thank you.

Creamed clouds overhead
wait to be bricked.

Sunlight.
All growls connect.

Sour
your own species.

Trap
cherry bombs.

Fuck the man
made of cloud.

Centuried light
falls through –

tending while slashing,
moving the burn.

To the Girl without Birds
at the Top of the Stairs

No heirloom will guide you.
Nor the dun-coloured rabbit.

Those dreams of missing the plane –
(Are the stars computing?)

When in doubt – hide.
Bury the purse dream

beneath your pillow. The lichen bear
will emerge from the rock.

There are other ways to hear a cry.
By swimming to a new poem

you push through the rough.
And to witness the dripping cloud

toughens skin.
Love happens in rain

and the hour is catching –
all that and just is.

pupa

Back to the Quarry

This surface for long-legged spiders
once absolved teen skin.

Plunge into the limestone museum.
Mingle with rusty machinery

sunken by a triggered spring.
Let sunfish nibble toes and raise

the fear of turtle snaps. Pursue
pathways craved by perch, catfish, bass.

Dive in. Turn to water before it freezes.

Katie's Appointment

There is a kitten on the ceiling.
Katie is dead angry about it.

A man has a gloved hand
in her mouth. She wants to bite it.

"Wider," he orders and Katie obeys.
She smells, with sniffles,

the Lux on his wrists,
the Brut on his neck,

scents of onion. Spearmint.
No man has been so close. Except

The Watch

Six foot three, basking in tawny heat,
sunk in his lounger, spring to September.

His face bakes like earth.
Chest hairs slice the sweat beads.

The black leather watch (he never forgot
to unstrap) ticks beside his ghetto blaster.

Cobalt eyes, silver thick hair, dentured smile,
arms folded under the crest of his chest,

he poses for fall's final mould.

*

Later – after the black skid, spin and deep
tip of the freshly polished blue Caddy;

after the crunch of skull on the dashboard;
even after the front-page photo and headline –

my father's watch, still ticking,
unzipped from the OPP's plastic.

No cracks, glass smooth to touch.
Dry mud flakes sprinkle like ashes

onto my opening hand.

Black Kettles

A leashed collie tugs like a kite.
Birds gather into bouquets.
Up ahead, the dirt road bends
as the neck of a swan.

Grief is like waiting for fifty
giant black kettles to boil.

Paper Dolls

Mute paper cut-outs
birthed from books.

Envious wardrobe
fastened by hooks.

Teeny torso.
Side-view sick.

Torn. Tattered. Tattooed. Trick.

The Doll Maker

after Olina Ventsel

Little Olina travelled by train,
her mother, lost, in Sakhalin,
her father in Siberian camps.
Arms, heads, hands, legs.

It so happened I trusted dolls.
Told them all my secret thoughts.
Dressed them up in fresh attire.
Loved me, quietly, leaning close.

Doll is the world. The magic stick.
The carried stick through place and time.
While making doll I feel each kick
until they break into a life.

Bye-Bye Kitties

Inside long boudoirs, dolls lounge and laze
recline like vamps on pianos, divans.

Smart set mascots of "The Charleston" days
accompany ladies on city streets.

Cinema magic, that's where it's at.
Bohemian Clara, the ultimate "It."

Lenci creates high-quality bodies,
exquisitely so, no flapper dare part with.

Until the crash. The well-to-do falling . . .
goodbye to dolls better dressed than they.

Eye-Flower

What was I before ascending the stairs?

Eyes lock at the top –
sclera, pupil, iris.

Do stamens matter?

Though we haven't met as yet,
blue eyes break into bloom –

cornflowers blossom in a crowded room.

The Hummingbird Lie
after Raymond Carver

Suppose I say, "Summer"
after finding *hummingbird*
written on paper next to your dresser.

You say, *It's nothing. It's not*
what you're thinking.
And then you lick the salt from your lips.

The Cutting Reason

I go back to the island,
see the house, no longer home,
breathe the sea, to breathe the sea.

Walking the streets, Belfast on Orange
Eve. The two of you, sipping tea. Bewley's.
Pane of glass, the glass between –

and when my skinned heart finally stops
beating and beating, a Lambeg drum,

I know, having walked away,
the cutting reason why I came.

You Are the Age I Was When I Met Him

So many times I have hugged you in my absence.
You became my right of way. The southern
door that took me north and put this house back in my
mouth.

Pteros

Now it's time. *Open*
your eyes.
Red petals strewn
across garden sheets.

We enter bloom.
Stems entwine.
And on our backs,
our twin thinning backs,

we feather. Red.

Imago

My life as larva has ended.

Silken girdle around my middle,
pupa blends with vegetation.

The greening gift of greener cloth,
my chrysalis – the last instar.

A swaddled change that can't be seen.
Internal systems rearranging.

Leather ripe, eclose my bind.
Shrunken leaf, laundry wet.

Pump in air, escape the crippling
drain of red. *It's time, it's time.*

Dew receives meconium.
Dawn, the quiet. Imago. Up.

the

red

element

Window Washer Sings at the Terminal

His song makes me think
of green hills with little green stalks
upright, wind leaning. Look.
He is a sparrow in those fields
trilling the echo of his lyrics,
flapping from blade to blade across
the panes of glass, the walls,
until he lands, easing. His song has edged us
to the clarity of sweet loss and the window
is ready now for wings to fly through it.

Pink

Pink is my tutu. My burr
scratch. Pink tights.
The pink of mother's
neck as she needles and whirs.
Singer. Petal faster. My tutu is flat and pink.
No perfect pirouette. *But I followed the instructions.*
Rip of stitches in her eyes as her pink
sandals pump the pedal. No, no, no,
that's her on the pink piano.
She is sewing my first pink tutu.
She is playing her scale of pink rain.
Allegro!

The Front Yard

Pink was out there breathing.
Pink and the cut of the mower
caught me. I left my doll
lying on the steps and ran
into the silence. Dad was on his knees,
peering. I crouched there.
Don't touch it. But my finger
felt something. That night
I dreamt my thumb purred with fur.
The next day, I'm told to stay inside.
The slam of the door
makes the face of a cat in my face,
parcels of pink on the red grass.

It's Only Her Piano Face

Sometimes I'd come home from school and find her playing.
Notes, little keys, covered my footsteps up the stairs.
I'd watch her long back swaying, until the long song ended.

One day, I pushed into her peripheral vision.
I saw her face crinkle like tin. The taste of foil between my teeth –
You're not my mother.

But I was a smart girl. I knew better.

Pufferfish

All swagger and bloat like a bully's memory,
the blowfish, air-stuffed in a child's basement
blows through me like the soft exhale of fuck.
Now I can forget all of our flotsam and jetsam, our spines and pricks.

The Art of Wrapping Cow Tongue

The pointillist pink slab
scrubbed with clover and cud
hangs in Bickel's freezer.

It receives my frame of Styrofoam
and saran to become
a bustle island skirt on a Sunday afternoon.

Pigeons

They coo and waddle and peck at stale bread.
They enter the sky like you can't do.
They nest on ledges of the Candy Factory Lofts
and pretend they are cliffs by the sea.

His Birthday Falls on Halloween

An airy hand carves a hollow
in your sleeping forehead and settles there.

When it lands on light's marrow, the lost bones of your brother,
all hell flickers through a crowd of orange mouths.

Like Snowdrops, Like Milk

If only he could.

After the ice-encased
coffined freeze,
if only he could unwind

to spring's slow release.
The cudding rain, the uddering sun –
milk through the giving dirt.

You in Haliburton

There is something that happens to you in Haliburton.
Your business skin disintegrates and your gait
mosses airily upward. You look taller in sneakers,
and your eyes sand whiter along the edges, no more
jigs of red. You sleep deeper in the hammock
of silence, wind-lulled or rocked by quiet, the colder
air a comfort to your white-collar lungs. You work
your body felling trees: saw, gather, stack. The smell
of wood a scarf round your neck. It ties you to this place.

The Ritual

Surrounded by green's dark, the day's wind
gathered in a knot, we walk the country road after dinner,
the flush of wine scoring our skin.
The tingle, after fireworks that we can't see,
hums through the palms of our hands.
We don't have to talk if you don't want to,
but we do in whispers when the woods blink back.
Brief, pale, yellow, we've arrived at the ritual. Come now. Right here.

Sighting

Fractures of light through the trees ripen her pelt to a time-lapsed apple.
She stares without twitch or blink until the sun
deers behind a cloud and she browns and she branches into the trees.

To the Weatherman

Tell me, will you ever really
predict the ripple of water?

Whether it rides stag-like
in a white antler roar

or lies quiet, a doe dreaming blue.
Face it, you will never know

if it's the stillness that moves you
or the moving that stills you.

Don

This scissor inside me – I felt it!
The swimmer swimming down my back.

He was alive when it happened,
moving through the house.

I listened. His steps were syllables.
His steps were the blue notes I jotted

down in my Hilroy. The spaces
were the whitecaps surging in our quarry.

The Terrible Pond

I often dream of terrible ponds,
frogs the size of Jack Russells.
The frogs turn into ponds,
ponds that bark like bugs in heat.

Sometimes I hear my mother's voice
locked in the water, churning the green,
calling me closer. Temperatures rise,
a cloud above the water, and when my eyes

look back at me, deeper pupils pulse
like passing sails, strips of mist
clouding the bars in the water. Mother,
I'm here, Mother. Mother, I'm here now.

winterkill

More Than Horse

They have forgotten the billy-goat beard,
the lion's tail, the cloven hooves.

Horse.
I am more than horse.

Conceived by the absence
of fears, my horn neutralizes poison.

I want to lie down on a virgin's lap
and close my lids inward.

But they would only take this as a sign.
My face, a walking steeple.

What Drums Through Him

Splayed and reed-fingered
he hangs against the cottage pane.
His belly drums through his neck.

We are nose to nose, me
and the frog I cannot name
without my Peterson Field Guide.

Yet what drums through him
drums through the rain, through
the glass, through us in our forest.

Turtles

I wanted something alive,
not stuffed.

Soft heads hinged to shells.
They glisten in the plastic pond

with the plastic tree.
Two. In the water.

Out of the water. They don't
notice me. What am I?

I am the storm.
I am the eye.

I let them stew in their piss.
I wanted something alive.

Partridges

The defuzzed needle made it clear.
Mom was in the hospital losing
her breast. We played it
at home. The first visit. My tongue
lay flat when he passed it to me.
I never threw a tantrum for it
like I did with those hourglass Barbies.
How did Dad know? He'd just
bought the milk we'd gone out for,
but here was the record I wanted.
On the label, five partridges
follow their mother in circles, forever.

Boy and Lawn

When I close my eyes, I see
the weeds through his head.

Clover. Dandelion. Wild carrot.
Daisy. I wanted every day

to be Saturday, for the grass
to grow high like the waiting

inside me. Dad paid the boy
to mow. I watched him

turn aisles through my
bedroom window. His glasses

thick and black. I saw
those eyes close up. Green

hovered between us
like the spears on his grave.

Fiona

Oh, I blame
my very sadness
on Fiona.
My lost smile
and my returning sadness
on Fiona's sadness
and her lost smile
that prompted the teacher
I loved to put down
her chalk and purr,
Oh, what's the matter,
my dear Fiona?
And all heads turned
away from me,
away from me,
and darkness roped
my folded arms
and tied a double knot
in my sadness.

Winterkill

Frogs bloat and rise
like hellsnow. They drank
all that the pondwater
held through their pores
and through their toothless
mouths. They breathed
the way rocks breathe
if rocks could breathe,
cloudblocked by ice
beneath the falling snow.

Escarpment

Trout lily.

Fins of teeth slitting the earth,
writhing with worms.

Jack-in-the-pulpit.

The man inside the hooded leaf
holding his voice for the gust.

O

how red petals come brutal
through the white trilliums of Niagara.

Lemon

In your wake the quarry shivers. O yellow star.
Pine tips rubbed with light, leaking light
like the slats of a painted gate. We sit on the dock.
Watch. The flat blue fruits from lemon to orange.
The blade of the day pierces us, then rests.

I Almost Laughed at Mother's Funeral

She's not in there.

The Buried

In a shallow grave of sand, done up to the nines in a huge flowery chiffon dress stretched out like a sail on a beach in the Hebrides, pecked to pieces by birds.
– Tilda Swinton, Eccentric Glamour

The breeze soothes the summer's
burning as it lifts off
the lake but the hot
sand holds the white heat
so we burrow our toes to find
the cooling. Bury me
in a shallow grave of sand.

I lie back and you shovel
beach over my pale
body. I let the itch of it
enter me. It's as if a thousand
insects have taken free rein
and clothed me in their stings. I am
dressed up to the nines

now, a level
away from all that I once knew.
A head. But when I close
my eyes I become
the buried.
A cloud passes over
in a huge flowery chiffon dress

and the sand is the smell
of my new skin. The grainy
case of my lungs pumps
through homes of crabs.
I am the sound
of the underneath
stretched out like a sail

in a photograph. I am pure
verb going nowhere.
Even the wind
can't move
me. The sand bars my body
from the water's rise
on a beach in the Hebrides

where time is carved back,
landlocked to the hours
of sand that has
no hours, only bones.
I'm not afraid
of you leaving; I'm only afraid of being
pecked to pieces by birds.

Usually I Forget These Dreams

I'm back at the quarry again.
It cliffs to a waterfall
and you dive down to where the dark
angles in. Now I can't find you.

The soap opera woman rows toward me
in her one-woman boat.
There, beneath the dock,
your red swimsuit, floating.

But you're safe. You surface.
A fountain erupts from your mouth.
You gulp the quarrelling air,
and your scales twitch back to skin.

My Ear Is Lost

My mouth won't *u*
the way Mademoiselle wants it to.

"Ew. Ew. Ew!"
Her face bullets to a freckle.

I taste her stale croissant on my tongue.
Tears take over. They talk for me,

sobbing the wrong vowel.

Before Recorded History We Waited /
Recorded History Became / The Occupants

A metal horse and buggy at the end
of a metal stake, hanging like a branch
that never changes and can't be chopped,
only lifted and replaced or not replaced.

Duck

The cries of all those lost
dogs are inside that egg
with the pure orange yolk.

Duck. Not hen yellow. Orange.
The yelps of lost dogs.

I Learned the Word *Mauve* from You

"She couldn't take the pinprick," you said.
Her right leg warped, wounded.

Already I felt fate turning. She lay
flat on your mauve bedspread.

The mauve light shifted the yellow
pigment of her skin in your hands.

"You have to give her back," I said.
As you eyed my new doll,

as I eyed the new walls.
"Mauve," I said, over and over. "Mauve."

Quarry

Real rocks once but they were all dug out.
My parents were real too, alive like the rocks
that are no longer real. See the blue field the osprey
sees before he rends the rock bass?
Water ruptures. Stills and holds. Water skaters
bridge across it. Blast. Dig. Quarrymen's work.
Dynamite arteries surround us as metal stakes –
core, quarry, *coeur.*

Moths

No pain yet. White cells
move as if in stocking feet,
heel and toe to bone and pancreas.

Lamplit, she sits smoking
on the Scotchgarded sofa,
looks out at nothing because it's dark.

The window is breaking
the sound of waves in the quarry.
The moths keep hitting the glass to get to her.

her

red hair

rises

with the

wings of

insects

Note:

Many of the poems published in *Her Red Hair Rises with the Wings of Insects* are responses to poems by the Irish poet Dorothy Molloy from her books *Hare Soup* (2004) and *Gethsemane Day* (2006).

Molloy died ten days before the publication of *Hare Soup* in 2004.

To the Animal He Met in the Dark

I've often thought about you.

How you came in the night, in the middle of the night,
to stand on the road for some goddamn reason.

How in the blinding light you stood as still as branches,
like anything trapped.

Nothing to see in the darkened windshield –
just the last expression on my drunk father's face,

and you, white-tailed beast, reflected, just like that,
on your way through your own nocturnal route.

I have so often thought about you.

Chthonic

after "The Woman and the Hill," Hare Soup

The lilacs have risen to solo in the corner orchestra of greens.
Purple odours permeate the branched alveoli of my lungs.
I slip through the briars, listen to wind shaking the canopy, stand
in place till I'm pulled through the port of entry.

I fight. Play possum. But my wit leaks as lilacs rust
from bone ivory. Death seeps. I hold
my breath to tease the light they say is coming,
but like *the trees I* darken *the forest.*

You must find the hidden passage inside the earth's purse.
Chewing worms. Burrowing owls! Nothing is still,
not even my mind turning to brain, a field in fallow. The earth
slides over my face. I see the exchange that's happening –

a dead mother wants out. Her red hair rises with the wings
of insects, and I sink further than *the lair of the fox.*

Gold Carp

after "I Saved Them in Mid-Winter," Hare Soup

Mint, weed and stone. Black water takes the night down
and darkness is held a hostage, a trap.

I think of the fish that swam in the quarry's inlet –
shallow pocket barred with light.

I never cared for fish but *I was quite fond of one.*
Torpedo gold. As still as the drowned floats alone.

Cornered for no reason. No aquarium as cage or
wall as trap. No toes to dip. No liquid to cup.

A hunch-backed carp, he used to raise my mood
when he mouthed the bread pellets.

Our images met at the hinge of our worlds.
Bottom-feeder. Bottomless sun.

Winter Broccoli
after "Four Haikus," Gethsemane Day

Not for the backdrop, but to enter green.
How should I place my foreign foot?
Already this land unlikens me. Blood-soaked
drumlins. The Antrim accent makes my inner ear *bleed.*

Oh, but the purrs of a pub in strings.
His voice slips through my sixth sense.
Medicinal split between this and this.
And he is so real. And I am so normal.

Purple hearts sprouting flowers in hedgerows carry
the glisten of sex as the night blows stars to deafen
our ears and we are safe beside the sea's deep
negotiations, *unseen in the forests of* our own taking.

I pine no more. My home is his skin.
But the ocean can't hold without Earth as container,
moon as pull. No oxygen in ether. Only stars
that fail to shape this *winter broccoli.*

Vow of the Grounded Tongue
after "Live Model," Gethsemane Day

In my mind I don't make the vow. Slip a stuffed horse
in my bed, make its head my head under the cotton sheets.

Night serves to even out misaligned shapes – *so I dress,*
slip the latch like an accomplished thief, go out the back door,
left unlocked. The house, a storm stay of sleep with me not in it.

Slumbering dreams float up the chimney's lip like ghosts
pining for skin. I *make my way down* the long gravel driveway,
past shadows of rabbits and shut-eyed birds; black trees shift

in dark shudders. The moon teases: I see you as I ascend
the stairs. At the click of the latch to your king-sized room – there,
curved in sleep, like the stuffed horse hiding my shape.

One lost self finds another as you rise, a crescent grin on your face,
and pat the place we know I'll fit. The click *of stiletto on marble.*

Between His Finger and His Thumb
after "How to See Wales," Gethsemane Day

The way the sun peeks out from a continent
of cloud, a geyser of light that rams the sea
and breaks all meaning into knuckling diamonds,
he gave me full instructions re *weather* once he knew
what I needed to know. Dumb as a round square,
I sat there while he sped the car over green hills,
the bleating sheep too fat to be clouds, too warm
to be snow. We rode through a tunnel of rock,
blasted to give route – back and forth each *season,*
light cloud cover over the sea. Always the clouds, even
at night. But the moon pushed the bloom
of the ivory in waves that rippled less than diamonds,
more like the glow of a spotlight we felt when we did
what we did, and the round moon entered and
took us in, like *the sun at an angle like this he showed me,*
and I believed him, even though he wore the evidence
of ceremony. But what's a band of hollow gold?
A ringless moon or a sun eaten by dark circles.
We saw the dark circles; we were the dark circles,
but who can see when the night is strung (between
his finger and thumb) and the sky just like that.

Riverbed

after "Fruits of the Womb," Gethsemane Day

I shudder to think that I once needed
the intervention of reason. The V of my lap
tingled *along the bikini line* where he opened me up
like a riverbed, the sheets surrounded
by sand and the rapid waves we made
beside the sea's flat rock that *yielded fibroids*
of moisture and moss. We grew a life
beneath the blanket. We fell like fruit after
August rain, pearling the dew of the aftermath.
Our rind, our doubling, *big as melons.*

Cloak
after "Sobs Rack My Chest," Gethsemane Day

I hide my power in a cloak I hoard as anger.
My jaw gears like a charging bull;
hairs horn from my butting forehead.

Stick of flame, I bring fresh heat
to a room like sun in *sky. There is no edge
from which to hang* your escape. I whore surrender.

Not bad, this giving up. No tit-
for-tat just a hit in the chest
where you slip between heartbeats.

Mushroom mouth.

Don't say I don't share *my plumb line. No ledge
on which to lay* your lost self? Give in
to my configuration. Hang on to a happy organ.

Be good and be dummy spewing out of my mouth.
Sing sweetly to *my spirit-level. And you are outside
piling logs* for relief. Even hunger needs a break.

Now let's pretend you're mad again. Committed
to a door with no handles; marionette strings
sting sharp injections.

And you'll keep coming back
because I keep you
working on your own wreckage.

Tourniquet

after "Ménage à Trois," Gethsemane Day

Nobody can say she can't beat him on the tennis court.
Her shots land safely on lines and chalk flies up in puffs
of surrender, but take him home and he's the official.

His whistle lives inside his mouth between the pink
of his teeth. Like a drawbridge she lowers *on a string,*
makes waves at the moat she can no longer cross.

Come back, come pull her up. She can't straighten herself
in her flattened state or feel his foot pumping her back.
She can't see a thing until he signals: over.

Cotton is cover – what clothes are for, and hair that falls
across forehead and shoulders. She knows the pain
a hospital hides like the red on her arm now blue now white.

She'll *make a tourniquet* out of his next attack. Then
one day he leaves. She is lying on the floor even though
she's standing up in the house of herself. Cornered, quiet.

Domestic

after "My Heart Lives in My Chest," Gethsemane Day

He sculpts my words with the chisel of his mouth.
Fits me inside his mind's binding. I do what I'm told
to get my playpen back, the edge of no to end
each *day. What did I do* to exit his eyes?
Blue-blinding marbles detached from the brain
that stems them. He won't answer. Sits
in his fat easy chair. What did I do *or what*
did I do not but wear something pretty? He spits
his words in blurry circles; hurls stones
of vowels at fields of bruises. Clothes
with round edges give too much of me to see.
"Who you trying to impress? Some fancy man?"
He's laughing now. "You think I'm serious? Just
want you to be safe, Pet." Blind *heart, pack up and run.*

Hat Rabbit

after "Death by Poisoning," Gethsemane Day

She left us waiting for the rabbit in the hat. How long
do you stare at a black top hat waiting for a rabbit
to hop out?   She was like our mother
for seven years. She never responds to our calls.
The blood that runs through us doesn't match;
we can't signal her homing.   *They* say she *left*
because our dad wasn't nice. The neighbours leave *us*
grief trees in their stares; we see the pity seeding their eyes.
So tempting to scoop the jelly out.   Or better yet,
to tap it like sap. Poor little orphans. We aren't orphans.
We have a father and a file of postcards, so we know
where she is: *wailing at the wall* in a distant country.
Magic isn't a trick. It's the return of
what you want. *And that was all.*

The Animal Game
after "Grandma's Zoo," Hare Soup

Now I'm a bird in the nest of your lap.
I flap my blanket of feathers.
Elongate my growing neck.

You take another one out, and I leap:
frog-green and slippery,
my tongue slides, ruler-long –

I aim for your fingers. You pretend
to dribble and present it to me.
It roughens my tongue like wolf teeth.

We feel the drumming tremble. Mean fists.
Our game is bruised.
Sit down. Your grandmother's coming.

The Bullied
after "Freed Spirit," Gethsemane Day

When I play invisible, the boy
sneers. I look away
and he's still looking.
His gathering of buddies
mock me with their yawn-traps.
You must learn how to look
and look back.

Can they see me now
when I press against the red brick wall
as they play *Planet of the Apes*?
I'm the lost thought inside the ocean
in Mrs. Easy's atlas.
How I'm gyred through the ether
is how God made me.

We are all icebergs to turn
green inside. Clouds hang
at half-mast. Another mother
is dying. The sun screams
yellow until the ding
of the recess bell. I fall in line.
Can they see in this stalk of wild fennel,

the twinkle of my silver buckle?
Big feet, they snigger.
I feel dot small. The crayon wave
on my paper rides the hair of water.
The scent of chalk is not home.
You pay a price when the cat's got your tongue.
Fire in the face, the cinder *and spark*.

Peas and Barbies

after "Barbie," Gethsemane Day

Make her naked and still she smiles,
exposing breasts without nipples.

Nipple.

We giggled at the word in the secret book
where the small arrow pointed.

Nipple.
We said it at the same time.

I made a doll of mashed potato
with nipple-peas on my plate.

Take charge *and spit.*
Witless move. Nana's looking.

Don't play with your food says the line
in her lips that melts the wizard in mine.

She blinks the nippled world away.
I give the world too much.

Fork more food in your mouth
and keep your eyes shut;

be an *empty-headed thing*
with shredded carrot hair.

Now roll on into Vegetable Land
where potatoes rule and peas shrivel

when told to stack up like tennis balls
on a Prince racquet.

Which one will tip the hill?
This pea. That.

"Eat your meal. It's getting cold.
You'll be hungry later."

I'll chew my *hair.*

"Nipple."

Jelly-Bean
after "Paulo Freire's Theory Revisited," Gethsemane Day

Now that he knows he can use his hands as hers –
that crush of attention snakes June through her winter skin,
makes minnows sun-flip through her stomach.

He *wished himself dead when he ate out her heart,*
but that's when she was beneath his moist sounds.

The thrum of his uncle blood quickens the trick
of the mind into a moan as *small as a jelly-bean.*
So small, they all refused to believe it.

Petals

Wrapped in the soft palate cloth of her throat,
her roughly smooth voice has gingered red,

and her palatine uvula hangs stiff as a stalactite,
as small as a finger without the half-moon nail.

It hangs useless and trapped as a fired trapeze man
and so unlike the deep roots she keeps burying –

the fractal limbs of the fragile plants and spring
flowers: the begonias, petunias. The rose. For what

emerges, emerges slowly despite the deadheading.
She sees her fruits lift from each finger-pinch,

and what emerges slowly grows between her soil-
covered legs into a ring of pink volcanoes.

The Queen Is Not Welcome Here

after "Gethsemane Day," Gethsemane Day

She won't leave, the Queen. She is hogging
my room, my living room. She is waiting
for me to leave my bedroom. And Bobby Orr
keeps waiting by the door, tapping his
hockey stick – a clock, a trick – Get out! I won't.

I cradle myself in my sheets, *the blood*
I am sweating rubs off . . . I hear the "Pomp
and Circumstance" playing outside
my chair-jammed door. She is hungry now,
her majesty. I sense it for the brass has stopped.

Her growls slip through the doorway slit,
quick pink contractions. I grab for the phone.
I holler, I'm coming! *but I'm still holding*
on to my head between the sheets. It hurts
even more with this receiver at my ear.

"They won't leave," I say to my daughter.
"Calm down, Mother. I'm coming over."
And the music starts up again to the tapping stick,
and the Avenger is waiting in his bowler hat,
his brelly's a tock to Bobby Orr's tack.

What cocktail is Daddy preparing for me? When
will my daughter open the door? I hear
my lost youth in her questioning voice.
I peek out the front – she is tossing a bag
down the garbage chute. I hear the long slide.

"Say goodbye to them, Mother." I won't. I can't.

The Night Prayer's Lord

after "'If I Should Wake Before I Die,'" Gethsemane Day

If I should wake before I die, I'll be in a box. I'll be
in the dark. I'll need a bell to ring – Oh, let me
be Victorian. My breath on glass. The wet stone
in your hand. Help me out of this coffin. Don't
let the woodworms in. Listen for the trapline going
knock knock. Help! Or *I'll take that beam out of my eye*
by cracking the oak. Let second chance surge
through me like a Greek chorus – saggy skin,
droopy eyelids, blue-veined hands, dryness
between legs, the nameless faces – *I'll sail a boat.*
I'll learn to fly! Reactivate adrenalin! Reap
the sown seed! Make life fit into the tunnel I have left.
Do all the things you don't do until the one day
there's nothing to do inside this massive oven.

Snowfall
after "Life Boat," Gethsemane Day

The snow holds light. Winter spins
into a trance. The sky can't keep up
with the falling. The sifting

edges in waves to the roof below the *pitch*
of night the white shoots up.
Ironed moon. Smooth as the dew

hidden in each flake, each crystal imprint
of pedigree lace. *Safe from the world, I hid
there all alone, till suddenly,* I'm falling –

pores – flakes – riding the white drift;
spin calm into a bleach explosion.
I stutter under the gathering spell and wait

for pain to level things out –
the weight of an animal's foot –
dark stirrings are welcome then.

Volume
after "S.O.S.," Gethsemane Day

Music looking for sound begins in silence.
She carried silence through the grace of our house;
carried her husband's talk, the silent place of his words
that stick like the alphabet magnets infesting the fridge –

letters a child needs to read through the silence.
I never heard her softly unwrap what she kept
fisted in her heart's lub-dub, lub-dub, lub-dub,
the red answer for the pump that stretched
oxygenated ribbons of air like *the sea around her,*
an underground current she carried from room to room –

silence that fell *like a shroud,* a tape of unsaid words.
Some of us are born for the hush of the seashell.
What to do when the quarry's uproar calls for us?
I refuse to be her silence. *My life* is *just too loud.*

Strawberries

after "Last Night the Itch," Gethsemane Day

No god smiles on sidewalk cracks around the quarry.
Only fossils like moles and freckles can shape a face
from rock. Tattoo curves are permanent.

Let my touch slip time between these *wild strawberries*
I picked for him in the goldenrod field.
Plump-ripe heads drank the sun into reddening.

Don't stuff so many in your mouth. But who
can resist? As poppies in a field, these *fairy*
berries are *a crop* of how much I love my father.

My tongue can move no language for that.

So I pick wild berries to soften the loss;
the one we no longer have; the dead red hue
that lives in the living-room silence.

I filled a whole thimble, right to the tip
of my thumb where her thumb used to sit
like a head in a hat, safe from needles.

The sewing is silent in her nook.
Clothes are store-bought now. No hands
like hers. A thimble's just *a silver container.*

My Skin Is My Grave

after "Bones," Gethsemane Day

Why should dying be news?
The bug is in the matchbox.
The shoebox holds the bird.
The first grave is our backyard.

And Mister Death, the high grotesque,
grins above. Aired in the room
before the earthworms' dark,
lidded and locked, my bones will be

like the cut tree, no longer expanding
in rings. Time skins me, and soon
my *bones will lose their marrow, but they're*
brave disintegrating; being change.

No longer serving their calcified
purpose, *they'll hollow themselves out*
for more sonority and air will song
through them as throats of birds.

There Is a Stir, Always

If I hold onto this body the snow will grow inside me
and the winter of my cells will flake
into tiny crystals like six-figured gods,
each arrow tip attempting to make the point of something
as tears flow.

There is a stir, always.

I rise to the cold
to take my place among the fragile stars,
and sleep.

the

celery

forest

Interrogation in the Celery Forest

We shoulder it onto the slab.
It squirms. Water. Electric-white.

Raindrops fast into absence.
No bridge as believable as all this.

Pliers were used. And absence.
A heart – skewered through skeins

of red nets and milk from some aimless
animal on the drowning cloth.

Now, intruder, bird's-eye, pip,
you must answer.

What Birds They Were

They arrive, a cloud with wings and a brain –
they soar and hover, land on the celery trees.

They cloak the leaves. Black fruit, seed eyes.
They become what they are –

human-watchers, staring at the frozen girl
strewn on the lawn. They drop

her temperature. She feels snow, her blue
lungs. Her mind floats – pastel clouds,

a glint of buckle, high and dry in the bird-free air –
she coils lightning into the double helix of herself.

Red-Eyed Vireo

You are difficult to find
among summer leaves, though I hear your song.

I place a pillow under my shoulder,
my arm behind my head.

Slowly, methodically, you scan the canopy for caterpillar prey,
I still can't see you.

I move the pads of my fingers
around my left breast.

From early morning to late evening, your incessant song,
the same question and answer.

I use light, medium and firm
pressure. Still, you're there.

Waiting for the Diagnosis

If we weren't holding hands, it wasn't
from fighting. No portent
on leaves, not yet. Only the Haliburton

Forest, full of birth – the Eden
we crave during winter's run. Then came
the scream. An animal – somewhere –

inside another animal's throat, followed
by that cold, testing silence we wore
as shivers, as scales, down our back.

The Pigeon Fancier

To fly them farther, faster, proves your bloodline's
tough. Sure, I embrace the widowhood system –
hens pre-race – they fuel the cocks.

I start them young. Month old, a few kilometres.
Then I tenderly edge them to over one hundred.
Not all come back – power line, Cooper's hawk.

Mink! Little shit tore a hole through the mesh.
Killed half. Left me with stiff,
bloodied birds. It couldn't eat thirty.

So, you start again. Breed a better bloodline.
Eliminate the weak, sickly, over-the-hill,
anticipate the heat from the flight on your hands.

Lake

You, dark waters, skimming the surface
of pebbles, the effect is breath,
not dark, you and your sand-wash
into thoughts of white, curling the rim,
your seeping stretches around smaller islands
and shores of crab boats landing north.

And so it goes. Again meets again –

Deciduous

Leaves dry out, become castanets, shaking.
Quiver. Tethered birds until one whispers – *Go!*
A sheet of starlings falls, winter's push.

Leaves curl, hands reach up –
take me back. No longer hidden,
abandoned nests in plain sight.

I see them everywhere after the diagnosis.
Black knots in X-rays – first
discovered by a circling hand.

They stay high in the air, waiting
for breasts that never come back.

The Fawn

Why the fawn with the missing foot?
She circles within the Celery Forest

as if it were a cage. She invites me in.
Her neck has thinned from my small hands

wringing the cotton silk. Her missing foot –
it shows me where the rain fits.

Beside the White Chickens

I have released the white chickens.
They are roaming on the moon.

They flurry past large doorways –
a release of matryoshka dolls

holding chickens within chickens,
waiting to be hatched –

to extend the red feeling,
to retract the red feeling.

MRI

No metal implants or fragments.
A long, fibrous stalk.
You signed consent, removed jewellery.
Face down through the doughnut hole.
Tapering into leaves.
Contrast material running through your veins.
Magnets. Pinnate to bipinnate with rhombic leaflets.
Still – lie still.
You've been given earphones, a padded table.
Seeds are broad ovoids.
Cushioned openings for breasts to hang.
Grown in an open garden.
Thumping. Clicking. Knocks and taps.
The celery's a cleansing tonic.
Whirs with car-accident screeches –
a father's skull, mother's mouth.
Wide range of cultivars.
The technician stands in a nearby room.
Inside, a seed; inside, a small fruit.

Winterhill

The heat glossing their backs. Moon licking the river

white. They thrive at night. Born nocturnal,
they smell the rub of dew slipping out.

To see through darkness blocked by moon, cloud, star.
Where is the water? The bullfrog knows.

The spring peeper. Their growing chorus itches the air.
There is no gate to pass. Just a metallic scent

they cannot detect. What hits, kills. Curled
into carcass, rot, on beds of gravel and dirt, they lie

ready to receive a birth of fly and maggot. But the lifting
fog is a trail becoming from the non-soul's heat, the organs' stop.

All instinct from inside them now furring air with whitish vale, shadow's
trick of weight. Here is where the dead live on – ghost animals –

in a world called Winterhill. They've become a floating pond,
a threshold of in-between, moist portal where water

finds water and fixes to air – *there, there.*

I Am One of 1,511 Patients Resting at Lakeshore Psychiatric Hospital Cemetery

My life is more important than my ghost.
The truth – orphan, spinster, Cottage D.
Floating through brick and other strange
appearances. A strangled curtain, light's trick.
It's cold being dead, being atoms in all
elements. Rumours of babies, fetus-deep
beneath the old working orchard means
apples and pears have faces. *Busiest*
haunt in the city. Patients and staff
never reported sightings. A ghost
is a fold in a slip of mind, frantic
nut of contagion. That fly at your neck.

Glass Animals

Their loud roar
resides in my room

where silence breeds
bars and gates.

Air can't split them open.
Glass animals know this.

Masks

Nature wore only one mask –
Since called Chaos.
– Ted Hughes, "Creation; Four Ages; Lycaon; Flood," Tales from Ovid

I entered Chaos through the plastic mask
of anaesthesia. Styx to bones that don't break,
just the lessening landscape beside a nipple
that never milked yet puckers pink. I need

a deeper slit on the left to secure clean margins
plus a sentinel undercut – hospital déjà vu,
a dawn re-entering as Sun dreams. No nail polish
on hands. Baby-naked beneath a stiff blue gown

falling open at the front without a pre-op grip.
How summer dissolves spring and autumn into masks
that seasons make from spin and tilt. I am made

more uneven above the heart. *Wake up!*
Maternal presence never felt since her Christmas
death. The age she died hiding inside me.

It Begins When You're Not Looking, Stops When You Are

My Kool-Aid is dripping, tomato soup's overcooked, clams with red sauce, leak week, Li'l Red, my little friend, joining the cast of *Pad Men*, on the blob, Crayola red, ninja red, Uncle Red, code red, Satan's baby, birthing a blood diamond, opening the floodgates, I'm having the painters in, surfing the crimson, riding the cotton pony, Carrie at the prom, rusty pipes, Miss Scarlett has returned to Tara, shark week, the Great Flood cometh, on the rag, the visitor, juice press, moon time, red wedding, on Wednesdays we wear pink, my bloody valentine, lining the drawers, Aunt Ruby is visiting, having a party at my pad, the Red Baron, experiencing technical difficulties, dredging the love canal, the server is down, the kitty is sick, expelling my hysteria, flying my colours, lady days, Mother Nature, T.O.M., ragging, "the regular discharge of blood and mucosal tissue from the inner lining of the uterus through the vagina" – air – air – end of sentence.

Shrike

Now come songbirds with hooked
beaks, eager for discarded body parts
trashed in plastic, coddled in blood.

With a feather-white apron down
their necks, masked with slashes
of night, they scoop, fly and fix

their finds on hawthorn branches.
Impaled, our tumours hang –
liver, pancreas, uterus, earlobe, breast –

thorns are for tearing off.
Tree in bloom. Sweet, savage
butcher bird, devour our cancers. Thrive.

Red Rain of Kerala

They said it could, it couldn't happen.
It came, they said, post–sonic boom,
post–crash of light, the raining red
that they said lasted till it stopped.
The beads of blood that wet the earth
returned as water to the world.
They said it was mammalian blood. A flood
of bats met meteorite. They called them spores,
red algae spores, red fly ash, red clay, fungus rust.

Breakwater

Pipe-staked, dynamite-stuffed limestone, blasted slabs
of fossil rock, time-press of ancient seas, sediments
snail into shellish shapes, creature tracks like hieroglyphics,
the cut rock – scooped and horse-carted out –
slowly, the hole fills . . . and up like an escaping creature,

a liquid cemetery air sac for abandoned machinery.
Hoofprints, bootprints dissolve to fish
inside the growing fluid. Water, now free to roam, softens
walls of its open-air cage, whitecapped, flat, cottonseed-coated,
leafed, sun-loved or winter-taken, the wait for forms to crawl out.

Sunrise with Sea Monsters
after J.M.W. Turner

Wide awake like a parent or spouse,
the worry, having inched
down my spine, crawls
into my mouth: Where were you?

    The sun rallies against this.
    Monsters make more from too many.

He stands at the front door,
a Breathalyzer sticker on his chest.
Floating letters gleam.
He did not pass.

    There is only so much light to make sea.
    To keep crew tasked to unfinished business.

Downcast, he stares at my fingers,
waiting for the wag and point.
Relief. My father's alive.
I shut my eyes to keep from waking up.

    Mine is a false cry behind scurvy clouds,
    where all the fevered brushstrokes have drowned.

Siren

I lure them to me with the milky
notes from my chest. Fools
will say suicide, unaware
of the sequins, the scales binding

ankles, knees and thighs, ending
two fingers below the pearl
of my navel. Freed
in new constraint, I swim –

sheathed by fish, their eyes vacant
as air bubbles. No void
for men to mine, to grunt
out their sex. They drown for me.

Egret

To see underwater. To see
through skin. To stab

at what moves is to reveal
your beak, the scissor, the incision

of scale to flesh. O vulnerable
heartbeat from being cut open –

no jacket to zip – just a steady
stitching beneath the whir

of mother's Singer from the drugged
language of my brain where the lawn

between the egret's pinhole eyes
becomes the grass I once walked on.

Sheet Music for Breathing
in the Radiation Room
after John Cage

Ratchet silence, I hear ammunition hammer.
Go on, health is a backwards trip. Yelps

before baby steps, tantrums, kicking candy
in the hourglass. Hex and melt each fixin'.

Toss the mulch of *yes*. Hush and play *4'33"*
under the spell she was. Don't melt. Don't.

Question the tunnel. Horse-throw black cattle.
Terraform black suns of stemmed plucked flowers.

Let mother's hands play trickster the bird before
a plenary nap. Let scorched petals fall at your feet.

A Leash of Deer

Untamable creatures, spotted as trout lily, camouflaged umber,
tawny, branched with satellite ears, air-cupped to the heartbeat of the ground.

Extended line between sun-dawn moon-dusk – a leash of deer.
Which site brought forth the first? Allowed leggy form to lift

up and off the forest floor into white-tailed leaps, or red, or roe.
No matter. Kill. Suffocation. Quick throat-slit. Kill and stop the leash of deer

from spreading out so when that fall night rears, a father driving home, one
road
away from home, no cloven-hoofed ungulate on Stonemill Road, parting from
a field

of parting corn, from stalk and husk and rustle beside a frog-thick croaking
ditch, to trigger
panic – the swerve – a father would have made it back to bed, exhaling Os of
alcohol through

greying shades of stubble, and a daughter would awaken to the muffle of his
morning
snores through cedar walls and not the 3:00 a.m. knocking at her bedroom
door, the waiting cop.

The Trick of Seeing Stars

The air between each bird is a flock
of anti-feathers, part of the migration, flow
of rolling air they navigate as water.

It's land that gives them trouble.
The full moon disappears. One thousand miles
and more. To be at ease in water, what grebes do.

A water bird is never wet. Their wings tire.
The full moon disappears. They view the dark
by city lights; it's like the trick of seeing stars.

Look up, you'll see each elongated body, neck
shaped into a boat, oncoming fleet. Smear
of city lights, the birds see water there, a temporary

stop en route to Mexico. Downing by instinct,
they extend their far-back feet and hit
the car-dark pavement – water birds are never wet.

Oak

If a lidded box doesn't announce *death*

a headstone will. Granite each visit.
Never bones, bones appearing as roots.
Just brush of wind, sun on hand.

Leave stone for flower.

But she keeps coming back,
the casket won't close, a beckoning
hand with gnarled fingers – roots

from underground
refusing to go underground.

Talk to her. Tell her –

It's time. Stop haunting me. I can't sleep –

You dream of trees.

Recurrence

Return to the Celery Forest. Accept the changes
in your sleep, unbroken dreams from the dead,

the built-in expiry date. When you are certain
the sofa's talking to the chair, hover –

Lily of the valley, a gladiola away from the catkin-drip sun
where air is birdsong and blue one rows across.

This hurts and it's meant to, the quiet of a final score.
Rain Brailles the window. I'll need a lifetime to read.

Acknowledgements

Many of the new poems in this book have previously appeared in various places. My thanks to the editors of the following: Arc Award of Awesomeness, *Arc Poetry Magazine*, *Belfield Literary Review* (University College Dublin), *Cypress: A Poetry Journal*, *Deep Time* vol. 2, Black Bough Poetry, *dusie: the tuesday poem*, *Exile Quarterly*, *Event* magazine, *filling Station*, *FreeFall* magazine, *Grain* magazine, *Here Comes Everybody* (University College Dublin pamphlet), Ice Floe Press, Ice Floe Press #*Geographies*, *Literary Review of Canada*, *The Malahat Review*, *The Montreal Poetry Prize Anthology*, *iamb: poetry seen and heard* (UK), *Pinhole Poetry*, League of Canadian Poets' Poem in Your Pocket 2021, *Soap Box* vol. 4 (*Light*), *The Quarantine Review*, *The Red House: An Anthology of Genre and Speculative Poetry*, *Stag Hill Literary Journal*, *talking about strawberries all of the time*, *Train: a poetry journal* and *Watch Your Head*.

Many of the previously collected poems first appeared in three books published by Insomniac Press: *Pupa* (2003), *The Red Element* (2008) and *Winterkill* (2010). My thanks to Mike O'Connor and the Insomniac team. The rest of the previously collected poems came from two books published by Wolsak and Wynn: *Her Red Hair Rises with the Wings of Insects* (2013) and *The Celery Forest* (2017, under the Buckrider Books imprint).

I am filled with tremendous gratitude to the editor of this book and indeed all of my poetry books, Paul Vermeersch. From our initial sit-down at Kilgour's on Bloor Street, which eventually led to my debut book, *Pupa*, to this milestone of a new and selected, I have benefited greatly from his unwavering support, guidance, enthusiasm and kick-ass editing. Thank you, P. I cherish this relationship. In addition to all of those acknowledged in my previous books, I'd like to thank the teachers, mentors, writers, family members, friends and students who have been part of my creative journey. Special thanks to Kathleen McCracken, Ayesha Chatterjee, Robert Frede Kenter, Bruce Hunter and James Wyshynski for their insightful comments and suggestions regarding the new poems included in this book. Thanks to my dear cousins Kristan Graham-Seymour and

Stephanie Gillingham and my *Hummmingbird Podcast* co-host, Jessica Outram. Thanks to the talented and dedicated Wolsak and Wynn team: Noelle Allen, Ashley Hisson, Jennifer Rawlinson and Tania Blokhuis. I'm grateful for this gorgeous book and all the others. Gratitude to Lorna Crozier for the beautiful blurb. This collection is dedicated to the greatest gift of my life: John Coates. Lastly, I'd like to thank my parents: Donald Graham and Mary Ellen "Rusty" Graham. Their untimely deaths unleashed my poetry journey. They are why I write.

Catherine Graham is an award-winning poet, novelist and creative writing instructor. *Æther: An Out-of-Body Lyric* won the Canadian Authors Association's Fred Kerner Book Award and was a finalist for the Trillium Book Award and the Toronto Book Award, while her sixth collection of poems, *The Celery Forest*, was named a CBC Best Book of the Year and was a finalist for the Fred Cogswell Award for Excellence in Poetry. A previous winner of the Toronto International Festival of Authors' Poetry *NOW*, she leads its monthly book club, interviews for By the Lake Book Club, co-hosts *The Hummingbird Podcast* and teaches creative writing at the University of Toronto School of Continuing Studies where she won an Excellence in Teaching Award. Author of *The Most Cunning Heart* and the award-winning novel *Quarry*, she has been a finalist for the Sarton Book Award and the Montreal International Poetry Prize, and has won the Miramichi Reader Award for Best Fiction and an IPPY Gold Medal for Fiction. Find her at www.catherinegraham.com and @catgrahampoet.